The Seven Natural Wonders

BY LISA FREUND

Table of Contents

INTRODUCTION

You are about to visit seven amazing places. These places are called the seven natural wonders of the world. They are places that astound us with their natural beauty, size, and power.

The Seven Natural Wonder

NORTH AMERICA

Grand Canyon

Paricutin Volcano

SOUTH AMERICA

Rio Harbor

Your trip will begin with a visit to wonders on land. Then you'll visit some water wonders. Finally, you'll finish your trip with a view of a wonder in the sky.

of the World

Northern Lights

Mt. Everest

EUROPE

ASIA

ERICA

FRICA

Victoria Falls

AUSTRALIA

ANTARCTICA

Great Barrier Reef

Wonders on Land
The Grand Canyon

The Grand Canyon of the Colorado River

Extreme FACT

The rocks in the deepest layer of the canyon are 2 billion years old!

The Grand Canyon is your first stop. It is a very deep **canyon** in the southwestern part of the United States. The canyon is a river valley with sides that are cliffs. Its steep walls were carved by the Colorado River. In some places, the canyon is so deep that three Empire State Buildings piled one on top of the other wouldn't reach the top.

In its towering cliffs you can see layers of rock stacked up like layers in a cake. These layers were deposited over millions of years. As the river cut through them, they became visible.

Everything in nature changes over time, including the Grand Canyon. Nature causes some changes. Wind, rain, and ice continue to **erode** the canyon. Careless tourists sometimes leave trash behind, and factories pollute the air in and around the canyon.

The many colors of the rock layers glow in the sun.

EROSION: ONE WAY TO MAKE A WONDER

How do canyons form? Little by little, the rushing water of a river washes soil away and cuts a channel. This washing away is called erosion. Given enough time, a river can wash away, or erode, even hard rock, bit by bit.

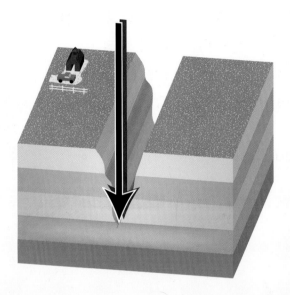

Over millions of years, the Colorado River cut a deep channel through the rock, making the steep cliffs of the Grand Canyon.

Wonders on Land
Mount Everest

Mount Everest

Extreme FACT

Mount Everest is growing! It gets nearly two inches taller every year. Why? See page 10.

Your tour now takes you to Nepal (Neh-PAWL), on the continent of Asia. Here you'll visit the world's tallest mountain.

Mount Everest soars 29,000 feet (8,700 meters). That's almost $5\frac{1}{2}$ miles (8.8 kilometers)!

Many people have died trying to climb Everest. Freezing cold, snowstorms, and falling chunks of ice make the climb very dangerous. The first climbers to reach the **summit**, or top, were Tenzing Norgay from Nepal and Edmund Hillary from New Zealand. They did it in 1953.

Tenzing Norgay and Edmund Hillary

SLIDING PLATES: ANOTHER WAY TO MAKE A WONDER

When you tap a hard-boiled egg on a table, the shell cracks into pieces. Like the egg, Earth has an outer shell. Earth's outer shell is called its **crust**. Over millions of years, the crust has cracked into huge pieces called **tectonic plates**.

ASIA

The plates move. They slide on a soft layer below the crust. Moving plates can make mountains. When two plates move toward each other, one may slide up over the other. That process formed the mountain range that includes Everest.

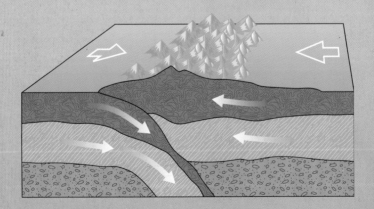

Wonders on Land
Paricutin Volcano

If your trip to Mount Everest left you feeling cold, your next stop should warm you up. You're going to visit a natural wonder that used to really "sizzle." It's the Paricutin (Pa-REE-ku-TEEN) **volcano** in Mexico.

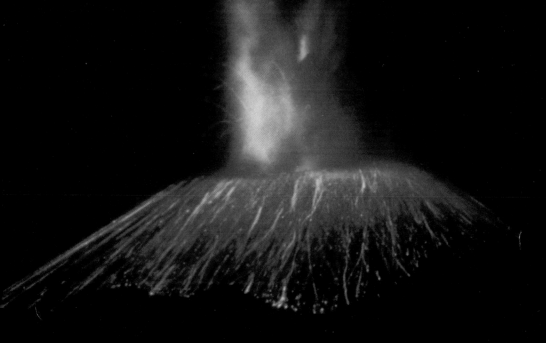

Paricutin destroyed two entire villages.

Most volcanoes are old. Some were formed millions of years ago. Compared with them, Paricutin is a youngster. It was born only 60 years ago. Many people saw Paricutin **erupt** for the first time. One farmer was standing very near the first opening that appeared!

Paricutin erupted for nine years. The hot **lava** sometimes shot high into the air. Now Paricutin is a tall cone of ashes, a sleeping giant that could erupt again someday.

Extreme FACT

People had to leave the village of Paricutin when lava began flowing over it. Many went to San Juan, a larger village farther away. In a few months, they had to leave there, too. When the volcano finally settled down, only the church steeples showed above the black hardened lava and ash.

Watery Wonders
Rio Harbor

The harbor at Rio de Janeiro

A lovely **harbor** awaits you in Brazil, a country in South America. Located in the city of Rio de Janeiro (REE-oh DAY Zhe-NAIR-oh), it is one of the best natural harbors in the world. A harbor may not seem like a natural wonder at first, but the amazing thing about this harbor is that it is so large, so beautiful, and reaches so far inland.

An unusual mountain stands tall beside the harbor. It is called Sugar Loaf. Its name comes from the fact that sugar used to be sold in molded shapes that looked like this mountain.

Unfortunately, the harbor at Rio de Janeiro is shrinking! People are pouring **landfill** into the harbor to make places for buildings and highways. If people continue filling the harbor, they could destroy its beauty.

Extreme FACT

The harbor is so large that it holds more than a hundred islands.

The tall mountain on the left is Sugar Loaf.

Watery Wonders

Victoria Falls

To get an idea of the size of Victoria Falls, notice the roadway on the right.

The next stop on your tour is the mighty Zambezi River on the continent of Africa. Do you hear the thundering sound of the world's largest **waterfall**? This astounding natural wonder is Victoria Falls.

Sliding tectonic plates and erosion helped form Victoria Falls. Two plates shifted to make the great drop of the falls. The waters of the Zambezi River crashed down. For millions of years, water raced over the rocks. It eroded the rocks to make the wide falls that you see today.

In the rainy season, more than 700 million cubic yards of water (540 million cubic meters) flow over the falls every minute. That's enough to fill 4 billion bathtubs—every minute!

People of the Kololo tribe who lived near the falls called them "the smoke that thunders."

Watery Wonders
Great Barrier Reef

Great Barrier Reef

Now you're headed "down under," traveling to Great Barrier Reef off the northeastern coast of the continent of Australia. It is the largest coral **reef** in the world.

Coral is a tiny animal. The animals live in **colonies**. When a coral animal dies, its skeleton turns as hard as stone. People call these skeletons coral, too. As the colonies grow and die, the pile of skeletons gets bigger. It forms a reef. A reef is a long strip of rock, sand, and coral close to the surface of the ocean.

How many kinds of fish can you count in this picture of a part of Great Barrier Reef?

It took millions of years for the reef to reach its present size. Coral reefs grow only about two inches a year. But it can take a lot less time to destroy part of the reef. Some parts are eaten by a type of starfish. Other parts are destroyed by careless people who walk on it or take pieces as souvenirs.

Extreme FACT

Great Barrier Reef is not a single reef but many smaller reefs that stretch more than 1,250 miles (2,000 kilometers). About 1,500 kinds of fish and 500 kinds of seaweed live in, on, or around the reef!

Wonder in the Sky
The Northern Lights

The Northern Lights

For your final stop on the tour of natural wonders, you'll travel far, far north to the Arctic Circle. Here you'll have a view of the amazing Northern Lights.

What makes the Northern Lights shine? The answer begins with the Sun. The Sun's energy is so great that it pushes huge clouds of gas out into space. Scientists call this gas rushing away from the Sun the solar wind.

The solar wind eventually reaches Earth. The solar wind has an electrical charge. The electrical charge makes some of the gases in the atmosphere glow. That glow is the Northern Lights.

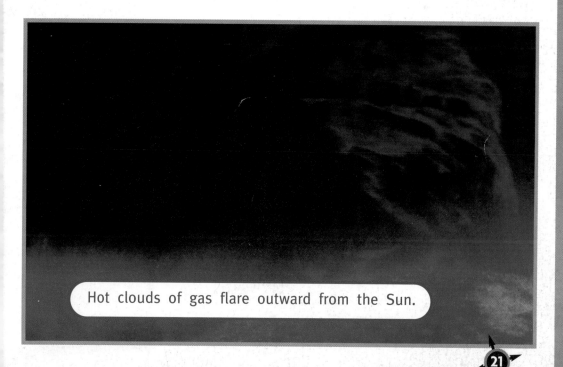

Hot clouds of gas flare outward from the Sun.

Point

Make Connections

Which special place would you add to the tour?

What makes that place a wonder?

The lights sway as if they were dancing. This movement is caused by shifts in the gases. The lights take on many shapes. They may arch across the sky like a rainbow. They may shoot across the sky in streaks. They can also look like flames.

Your tour has come to an end. You've visited natural wonders on land, water, and in the sky. Which was your favorite? Why?

Extreme FACT

In some places, the Northern Lights are so bright that people can read by them.

GLOSSARY

canyon
(KAN-yuhn) a deep valley with steep cliffs on both sides (page 5)

colony
(KAHL-uh-NEE) a mass of people or other living things in one place (page 18)

crust
(KRUST) Earth's hard outside layer (page 10)

erode
(ee-ROHD) to wear away (page 6)

erupt
(ee-RUHPT) to throw melted rock, dust, and ash out of a volcano (page 12)

harbor
(HAR-bur) a sheltered body of water along a coast that provides protection for boats and ships (page 13)

landfill
(LAND-fil) material, often trash or dirt, piled up to make new land to build on (page 14)

lava
(LAH-vuh) the hot melted rock that comes out of a volcano (page 12)

reef
(REEF) a ridge on the ocean floor that reaches to the surface; may be made of coral (page 17)

summit
(SUM-mit) the top or highest point (page 9)

tectonic plate
(tek-TON-ek PLAYT) a very large sheet of rock that makes up Earth's crust (page 10)

volcano
(vol-KAYN-oh) an opening in Earth's crust through which melted rock, dust, and ash are thrown out (page 11)

waterfall
(WAW-ter-fall) a place in a stream or river where water falls from a high place (page 15)

INDEX